Seven Stages of an Affair

A Play

Lorraine Forrest-Turner

A SAMUEL FRENCH ACTING EDITION

FOUNDED 1830

SAMUELFRENCH-LONDON.CO.UK
SAMUELFRENCH.COM

FOR AMATEUR PRODUCTION ENQUIRIES

UNITED KINGDOM AND WORLD
EXCLUDING NORTH AMERICA
plays@SamuelFrench-London.co.uk

020 7255 4302/01

Each title is subject to availability from Samuel French,

depending upon country of performance.

SEVEN GOLDEN DRAGONS

The play was first performed at Calday Grange Grammar School, West Kirby with the following cast:

Chris	Daniel Meigh
Gary	Silas Edmonds
Barry	Mark Knoop
Rob	Geraint Waters
Steve	Michael Green
Matt	Roy Tilston
Ben	Nicholas Lee
Chief	James Foggin
Crobo	Thomas Fitzpatrick
Garbo	Nathan Curry
Limbo	Richard Hawkins
Snorbo	Andrew Thomas
Rainbo	Michael Cavanagh
Grimbo	Ben Robinson
Znakbar	Daniel Roberts
Porc	Ian Dyson
Snorc	David Tucker
Gorc	Mark Burgess
Torc	James Greaney
Skworc	Julian Moss
Forc	David Jukes
Wakelam	Carne Simpson
Pilots	Piers Williamson
	Stuart Cassie

and

Mark Davidson	Geoffrey Drake	Geoffrey Gotts
Mike Tucknott	Marc Stephens	Mathewe Pollard
Christopher Frost	Pat Flanagan	Jim Corrigan
Stephen Powell		Jacob Hill

CHARACTERS

Chris
Rob
Steve
Gary } the Golden Dragons
Matt
Ben
Barry

Znakbar

Porc
Snorc
Gorc } Orcs
Torc
Skworc
Forc

Chief Elfling
Crobo
Grimbo
Gazebo
Limbo } Elflings
Snorbo
Trumbo
Garbo
Rainbo

Ben's Father
Gary's Mother

Pilot 1
Pilot 2
Hijacker

Wakelam, the wise old man

Bacillus
A Giant
Invisible Creature
A Gripper
A Glinch

Elflings
Orcs
Slaves

SYNOPSIS OF SCENES

ACT I

ACT II

Songs

ACT I

1. Peace and Love and Flowers and Music	Elflings
2. When You're An Orc	Orcs
3. Don't Be So Wet	Znakbar
4. Legend of the Golden Dragons	Elflings
5. This Is Our Chance to Be Heroes	Chris & Dragons
6. Join My Team	Znakbar
This Is Our Chance To Be Heroes (*reprises*)	Chris, Matt and Pilots, Dragons (excl. Steve)
7. Stand Up For Yourselves	Chris and Dragons
8. We'll Be Back	Znakbar and Orcs

ACT II

9. It's A Scream	Znakbar and Glinch
10. Celebration Anthem	Elflings
11. Watch your Step!	Elflings
12. This Will Be Our Quest	Chris and Dragons
13. Fight! Fight! Fight!	Elflings, Chris and Dragons, Znakbar and Orcs
This Is Your Chance to Be Heroes (*reprise*)	Chris and Dragons
I Am Back (*reprise*)	Znakbar
This Will Be Our Quest (*reprise*)	Company

The piano/vocal score is on sale from Samuel French Ltd

PRODUCTION NOTES

Cast

Although the characters are referred to as "he" throughout the script, reflecting our original production, there is no reason at all why many of the characters should not be female. Elflings, Orcs and other fantastic creatures are sexless and a production in which Znakbar and the Orcs are played by girls would have an interesting new dimension. I think to make the Golden Dragons themselves female would mean major alterations to parts of the script but feel free to try.

The size of the cast can be varied considerably. There can be large numbers of Orcs and Elflings or you can restrict yourself to the named characters. There is the possibility of doubling in the minor roles (e.g. Dad, Mum, pilots, hijacker, monsters, slaves etc.) allowing a minimum cast of 25–30 but, if you want to include as many people as possible, over 60 could be usefully employed. A large cast will give the songs more impact and make the crowd and fight scenes more exciting.

Music

You have two options. You could settle for a piano accompaniment for all the songs. This has the advantage of simplicity and makes life easier for the singers. Alternatively, however, several of the songs, as is clear from the score, are intended for a rock group of guitars and drums. This will be more exciting but does mean that the singers will need microphones with all the problems they bring. If you choose the latter option, make sure the singers have sufficient time to rehearse with the microphones. Even good singers often have problems with them initially.

Set

Because the scenes are short and the action moves quickly through a wide variety of locations, elaborate sets (with the resultant long gaps between scenes) are not recommended. Our production had a plain black set with the different locations suggested by a few items which could be moved on and off quickly and easily (a papier mâché boulder, a tiled wall for the changing room, a rack with clothes on for the shop). Background sound effects, too, can be very useful in suggesting a location (e.g. riverbank, airliner, football match, the wood).

Costumes

The costumes in the "real" world are mostly obvious. The fantasy characters should be dressed as in the many fighting fantasy/sword and sorcery books and magazines that are readily available.

Our Golden Dragons wore black swimming trunks, two bands of leather criss-crossed across the chest, short white capes and golden helmets (made from plastic bowls with wings attached and painted gold) which gave much opportunity for comic business (wings dropping off, wearing them back to front, falling over the eyes etc.).

Znakbar and the Orcs wore black leather, studs etc. with Znakbar sporting a Dracula-style cloak as befitted his higher status. Rubber gloves painted silver and with talons attached to the ends of the fingers, green make-up and blacked out teeth completed the effect. Long green hair is also effective.

The Elflings wore fur tunics and boots and each was made up in either red, yellow or orange except for Rainbo who, as his name suggests, was multi-coloured. Pointed ears are also a possibility. Decorations of flowers and bells help to give a 1960s Flower Power feel.

Effects

All the effects in the play can be executed very simply if required or, if you have the facilities, can be as complicated and elaborate as you wish.

Disappearing/Appearing
The script calls for several characters to appear and disappear. If you want to use trap-doors and flash boxes please do so but we simply had a very bright white light shining absolutely vertically down onto a small area of the stage where all the appearing and disappearing took place. At the appropriate moment all the other lights were blacked out leaving just this eery light. The actor then stepped out of (or into) the lit area to the accompaniment of a weird (preferably comic) sound effect and (dis)appeared. After a few seconds the normal lighting returned and the scene continued. This was both effective and amusing but it needed careful rehearsal with the lighting operators.

Monsters
The Gripper—as the text suggests this is a giant tea-bag made out of sheeting. The operator should be as tall as possible as the bag has to be made to measure and there must be room for Matt to fit inside with him when he is "eaten".

The Giant—he could be one actor on another's shoulders, an actor on stilts or platform shoes or just a very tall person.

Bacillus—a reasonably realistic bull's head is required here to create a minotaur-like effect.

Glinch—there is an opportunity here to create a very elaborate "show-stopper" of a monster. If resources are limited, though, a simple metal framework with a hinged mouth (large enough to feed an actor into) can be covered in sheeting or papier mâché and painted to look scaly or otherwise monstrous. Its appearance is up to you but I think a large blob-like creature which is mostly mouth looks best. A microphone inside is also useful to prevent his song being muffled.

Invisible creature—this effect is explained in the text. Dim lighting essential!

ACT I

A Clearing in the Forest

Various Elflings are engaged in gentle and artistic pursuits such as painting, playing flutes, and basket-weaving. They wear beads and bells. Gentle, artistic music plays

Song 1: Peace and Love and Flowers and Music

Elflings   Peace and love and flowers and music
Tranquil pleasures, easeful hearts
Dedicated to the culture
Of the civilising arts.

Rainbo, a dissident, punk elfling steps to one side of the group

Rainbo   Peace and love and flowers and music
Life is bliss here in the sun
That's if sitting watching grass grow's
Your idea of having fun.

Elflings   Peace and love and flowers and music
Bells, beads, joss-sticks, kaftans, mirth
Rainbo   For a geriatric hippy
It's a paradise on earth.

Elflings   Peace and love and flowers and music
Crosby, Stills and Nash and Young
Rainbo   Nettle wine, organic muesli
Wholefood pancakes made from dung.

Elflings   Peace and love and flowers and music
Life is bliss here in the sun
Where the songs of Scott McKenzie
Will forever linger on.

                  Peace and love and flowers and music,
Peace and love and flowers and music,
Peace and love and flowers and music.

Repeated until, unnoticed, a group of Orcs arrive

Porc Ah, look at the little elflings.
Snorc Yeh, aren't they cute?
Gorc Which one shall we disembowel?

An Elfling spots them

Grimbo Orcs! Flee!

They exit except for one, Crobo, whom the Orcs manage to capture

The Orcs tie him up

Porc Now, we wish to speak to your chief. You will show us where he can be found.

Crobo No. No. These are our lands. You have no right to come here. I will not help you. Never.

Snorc Perhaps *this* will loosen your tongue!

With a dramatic gesture he produces a hideous-looking weapon

Crobo Well, you go through that clearing and then just past the second rock there is a cave in the mountainside which leads through a secret passage under the mountain to our village.

As Crobo speaks the Orcs hurry him off

Black-out

SCENE 2

The Elfling Village

The Elflings gather agitatedly around their Chief

Grimbo ... and it was not until we were sure that they were not following us that we noticed that Crobo was not with us.

Chief They have captured him?

Grimbo Or worse.

Chief I am to blame. Since the feast of Apple Blossom six have been taken.

Grimbo But what can we do?

Chief We must no longer venture beyond the mountain.

The Elfins give expressions of protest and disappointment

I know that there the springs are sweet and the air is rich with the fragrance of the Amplona blossom but there is also great danger. The Orcs will not rest until they have discovered from us the secret of the magic ring of Magor and this they must never do.

Grimbo Can no one help us? Could this not be the time when the Golden Dragons are to come to our aid?

Chief The Golden Dragons, yes, the ancient legend of our people. I fear these are stories for children, Grimbo. It is many centuries since we have used the ring to summon help. Who knows if the tales are true?

Grimbo Try the ring. Let us find out.

Chief This is not the time. The power of the ring is only to be used in an hour of great need.

Grimbo What greater need than now?

Chief The Orcs cannot harm us if we do not venture out. Here with the mountain for protection we know that we are safe.

The Orcs enter with Crobo

The Elflings scream and run off except for the Chief who hides behind a rock

Gorc Listen, elflings. We have captured . . . What's your name?

Crobo Crobo.

Gorc (*in disbelief*) Crobo? We have captured . . . You can't be called Crobo. We have captured Crobo. Unless you reveal to us the secret of the magic ring of Magor, Crobo will die.

Chief Have mercy. We know nothing of the magic ring of which you speak.

Gorc The ancient writings clearly tell of how the mighty wizard, Quentin, entrusted the secret to your ancestors in the old time before the great darkness.

Chief Yes I know, but we seem to have mislaid it.

Gorc You cannot deceive us. Speak. And quickly. Or Crobo dies horribly.

He points to a box which Porc opens revealing a very small black blob

Chief You would not!

Orcs (*together, sing-song*) Oh yes we wou—ould!

Gorc I see you recognise the creature. The fire beetle. One bite from those tiny jaws and Crobo's doom is sealed. The most awful death imaginable as the poison pours through the body turning every vein into a river of fire. Death comes as a relief. This is your last chance. The secret of the ring!

Crobo I think he means it. You'd better tell him.

The Chief lowers his eyes

Gorc The fire beetle!

Porc opens the box. With tongs they place the fire beetle on Crobo's foot. It slowly starts to crawl up his leg. It makes a snuffling noise

Crobo Tell them! You must tell them!

Gorc Tell us and his life will be spared. Quickly, the fire beetle is an angry creature and will not wait long before its bite.

Chief I beg you. We know nothing.

They all stare at the beetle as it moves up Crobo's leg and onto his chest. As it reaches his shoulder, it bites

Crobo Aaaaaaah!

He writhes in agony in a spectacular manner before dying

Gorc Such will be the fate of all who defy the will of Znakbar.

Other Orcs repeat the name in a hoarse awed whisper

Orcs Znakbar!

Gorc hands the tongs to Porc signalling him to replace the fire-beetle in the box. Porc looks but it has gone. They all look nervously around for it

Gorc We will leave you now to think on these events. We will return each day and each day one will die until the mighty Znakbar . . .

Orcs Znakbar!

Gorc . . . holds the power of the ring.

The Orcs start to exit as the music for Song 2 starts. Elflings begin to come forward. The Orcs return suddenly and snarl at them. The Elflings dive for cover. The Orcs, rather surprisingly, burst into song

Song 2: When You're An Orc

Chorus

Orcs
You'd think it was
Our fault to hear
Some people talk
You've got no choice
You *gotta* be nasty
When you're an orc.

Porc
You got school, *you* got exams
You got careers advice
Well, let me tell you, buddy
You sure got it nice.

(*Speaking*) Do you remember when we were little Orclets, Snorc?

Snorc Yeh.

(*Singing*)
We had love, we had feelings
We had fine attributes
But 'cos we weren't too pretty
They thought we were brutes.

Orcs
You might want to improve relations   (but)
You gotta resist all those temptations
You gotta live up to expectations
When you're an Orc.

Forget all those lofty aspirations
Because you're under an obligation
To preserve your seedy reputation
When you're an Orc.

Chorus

Snorc (*speaking*) What is it we're really looking for, Gorc?

Gorc
Tenderness and affection
Cuddles, kisses and hugs
But 'cos we look like we do

We're branded as thugs.

Orcs   If you try to lend a helping hand you
Bet your life people misunderstand you
You *can't* carry on like Julie Andrews
When you're an Orc.

Chorus is then sung two or three times as they exit

The Elflings slowly return and gather sorrowfully around the body of Crobo

Lights fade to black-out

SCENE 3

A Changing Room

Chris Seven–nil. (*Louder*) Seven–nil!
Steve (*off; in the shower*) Forget it.
Chris That is the trouble with this team. You don't care about winning.
You just play for fun.

*Rob, Ben, Matt, Gary and Steve emerge from the shower, dry themselves
and dress during the following*

Rob I thought that was the idea. Bit of fun on a Saturday morning.
Ben Fresh air. Exercise. Keep fit.
Chris No. No. No. The only point is to win, to pound the opposition, wipe
them out, show them who's the best. (*He undresses*)

Chris goes into the shower

Matt We know who's best. Every other team in the league except us. We
haven't won a match in two years.
Gary So what? We have a laugh, don't we?

Howl of anguish from Chris in the shower

Steve What you doing this avvy, Rob?
Rob Wedding.
Matt You're not old enough, are you?
Rob I am *singing* at a wedding. All Saints. You know . . . it's a church. One
of them buildings with a point on the roof.
Matt On a *Saturday* afternoon?
Rob Listen, it's good money.
Matt You get paid? I thought you did it voluntary like. Any places going?
Rob It's a choir, not a heavy metal band. You have to be able to sing.
Anyway, you're going on holiday this afternoon, aren't you?
Matt Yeh. Malaga. Got to get home. Going straight to the airport after
lunch.
Steve See you, Matt.

Matt exits

Matt Bye.

Steve (*shouting into the shower*) What are you doing this afternoon, Chris?

Chris (*off*) Well, I thought we could all go to the park, do some training—ball skills and we could practise some shots. You need the practise in goal, Ben.

Ben No chance, Chris. I've had enough football for today. I'm going fishing with me dad.

Steve I'm going to Anfield to watch a *real* game.

Chris (*off*) Watching! Watching! It's playing that matters. Is it just you and me then, Gary?

Gary Sorry, Chris. I promised me little brother I'd take him into town. He got a record token for his birthday.

Chris (*off*) Your little brother! It's no wonder we're bottom of the league with this kind of commitment. A vital opportunity to practise and how many of the team will be there? One! Me!

The others have dressed and exit, taking Chris's clothes. When they have gone, three Elflings appear

Chris talks on unseen in shower

Chris (*off*) What you lot don't seem to realise is that you get nothing in this world unless you work at it. That's what these other teams do. Two or three nights a week they practise. It's nearly a month since we had a practise at all—and then you all wanted to be home in time to watch *EastEnders*. You get nowhere in this life unless you fight.

He emerges from the shower, with a towel around his shoulders and one around his waist (concealing his Golden Dragon costume). He doesn't see the Elflings. He looks for his clothes

Fight! Fight! Oh, come on, what have you done with me clothes? I don't know what you find funny about ... (*He sees the Elflings*)

Grimbo Greetings.

Chris Er ... yeh ... greetings. Is it the pantomime you want? I think they have the rehearsals in the church hall. It's across the ...

Gazebo It is you we have come to seek.

Chris Me?

Grimbo You are one of the Dragons, is it not so?

Chris Yes, I'm a Dragon, the captain actually. You haven't seen my clothes anywhere have you? Do you want to join the Dragons? You're rather small but I'm desperate. If you're any good ...

Grimbo He is the one. Quickly.

Gazebo We need your help. Touch this ring. (*He holds the ring out*)

Chris I'm not with you. Do you ...

Gazebo There is no time. Please. Quickly. Touch the ring.

Chris OK. OK. But what ...

Chris touches the ring as do the other Elflings. Flash. Smoke. They all disappear

Black-out

SCENE 4

Znakbar's Lair

The Orcs enter, looking rather nervous. They whisper and push each other

Torc O mighty Znakbar!
Orcs Znakbar!
Torc We have returned from the village of the Elflings. (*He falls to his knees and bows low*)
Skworc O mighty Znakbar!
Orcs Znakbar!
Skworc We have taught them to respect thy mighty power. (*He falls to his knees and bows low*)
Forc O mighty Znakbar!
Orcs Znakbar!
Forc The Elflings tremble at thy name. (*He falls to his knees, and bows low*)

Long pause. Orcs raise their heads, look at each other, grimace, nudge

Torc (*quickly, apprehensively*) But we didn't actually get the ring.
Skworc (*quickly*) Yet.

Fanfare

Znakbar appears. He is very small and wears black leather, studs, chains etc

Znakbar What!! What did I send you to do! (*He hits Torc*)
Torc To get the ring of Magor, O mighty one.
Znakbar Where were you supposed to get it? (*He hits Skworc*)
Skworc From the Elflings.
Znakbar *How* were you supposed to get it? (*He hits Forc*)
Forc By frightening them.
Znakbar *Wrong!* (*He hits Forc again and adopts a wet voice*) "By frightening them". (*Fiercely*) Not by *frightening* them! By *torturing* them. By *killing* them.
Skworc We killed one of them.
Znakbar (*going to Skworc and hitting him*) One of them! *One* of them! What's the good of that?
Torc And we said we'd kill one every day . . .

Znakbar goes over to him

(*Hesitantly*) . . . until . . . they tell us . . . where the ring is.

He cringes. The blow comes

Znakbar One every day . . . one every day . . . pathetic . . . how long do you think that's going to take?
Forc A week or two?
Znakbar *Shut up!* (*Hitting him*) I do not intend to wait any longer. That ring will give me the power I need. I have told you this many times. You know what I am. What am I?

Torc You're a b . . .

Skworc quickly claps his hand over Torc's mouth

Skworc You are hungry, O mighty Znakbar.
Orcs Znakbar!
Znakbar Hungry for what?
Orcs Hungry for *power*, O mighty Znakbar.
Znakbar Look at you, pathetic fawning creatures. I should have known better than to send you on a job of any importance. You couldn't strike terror into a child. Could you? Could you?
Torc Er . . . well . . . a child? . . . Well, I think we could . . . how big a child.
Znakbar Oh? Oh? You disagree with me?

Torc and Skworc shake their heads vigorously

We'll see. Look. Look. There's a child. (*Pointing to a child in the audience*) Go on. Frighten it.

The Orcs look nervously at the child

Go on! Let's see you strike terror into its heart.

The Orcs go and stand by the child not knowing quite what to do

OK. Come on. My terrifying henchmen. There it is. It's only small. Make it cry. Go on.

The Orcs growl, pull faces and make other feeble attempts to make the child cry

I'm waiting. I'm waiting. You don't seem to be having much effect. Go on. Pull out all the stops. Do your worst. It's all covered by the insurance.

They make further feeble efforts. Finally Znakbar batters them back onto the stage

Oh, give up. Give up. You're hopeless. You've no idea how to be evil. You'd think with my example to follow you would be exquisitely vicious but no . . .

Song 3: Don't Be So Wet

(*Singing*)   I sent you out to put the Elflings in a scare
They'd be more scared by a cuddly teddy bear
I sent you out on an execution raid
There'd be more dead if I'd sent the Boys' Brigade.

Chorus

        Don't be so wet, don't be wet, don't be so wet
        Don't be so wet, don't be wet, don't be so wet
        Don't be so wet, have you got the message yet?
        Don't be so wet, don't be wet, don't be so wet.

He pulls out a water pistol and squirts the Orcs with it

I want to hear where to find the magic ring
You come back here without finding anything
I want to hear how many Elflings you've impaled
You crawl in here just to tell me that you've failed.

Chorus

He produces a soda siphon and squirts them again

I sent you out to get those Elflings in your grips
(To) rip them to shreds not to forge relationships
I sent you out with swords, axes, knives and whips
Don't be so wet and you might not be such drips.

Chorus twice

The Orcs cringe as Znakbar drags on to the stage a stepladder, climbs it and soaks them with water from fire buckets, water bombs etc

Black-out

SCENE 5

Elfling Village

The Elflings are having a council meeting

Chief I fear that we must leave the village.
Garbo Where could we live?
Limbo There are the Caves of Firedor.
Trumbo Live in the Caves of Firedor? Forever in darkness? Only able to come out at night to gather food? I would rather die.
Garbo The Orcs would find us there. It would not be safe. Nowhere is safe.
Limbo It may be that Grimbo, Snorbo and Gazebo have found the Golden Dragons. They will save us.
Chief The Golden Dragons have not been with us for many centuries. I fear they will not be found. A legend—nothing more.
Trumbo Then we must resist for ourselves. When the Orcs return to kill one of our number, we must say, "No."
Limbo Say, "No?"
Trumbo Yes. Stand up to them.
Garbo But we are not warriors. We are peaceful and artistic and cute and furry.
Trumbo In times like these, Garbo, we must summon up from our hearts the courage that lies there, the indomitable spirit of our people, the spirit that brought them to this land in the time of the great darkness, the spirit that fought the unknown dangers, that faced the hazards of the Black Mountains, that forged a new home for us here in the Blossom Marshes. It has long lain dormant but I know that here, deep in all our hearts, we can find the heroic courage of our ancestors.

Grimbo, Snorbo, Gazebo and Chris appear onstage in a flash

Other Elflings all scream and run

Grimbo (*to Chris*) Our people. They are afraid of everyone and everything.

Gazebo Fear not! Our quest was successful. Behold, the leader of the Golden Dragons!

Elflings come forward jubilant, kissing Chris's feet. He is dazed

Chief Welcome. Welcome. (*To others*) Prepare a feast. Music! Let us celebrate the return of the Golden Dragons, ancient champions of our people.

Chris I ... er ... where ...

Chief Please be seated. Bring food. Bring wine.

Chris I don't think I understand.

Chief Where are our musicians? Let them sing the ancient anthem of our people, sung in honour of our ancient protectors—the Golden Dragons of Egremont.

Song 4: Legend of the Golden Dragons

Elflings
In the ancient times
In our ancient rhymes
The stirring tale was told
How a gallant band
Came to save this land
In those dangerous days of old.

Chorus

The seven Golden Dragons, golden, bold and strong
Seven Golden Dragons, golden, bold and strong
Seven Golden Dragons, seven Golden Dragons
Our heroes, our legend, our song.

Back then life was harsh
In the Blossom Marsh
Helpless against our foes
In that evil hour
In that tyrant's power
Came to us seven bold heroes

Chorus repeated twice until interrupted

Chris I think there's been a mistake here.

The Elflings laugh happily

All this about the Golden Dragons ... it's not ... you see ... the *Golden Dragon* is a pub ... they sponsor us ... we're a football team.

The Elflings laugh happily

You don't understand. You've got the wrong Golden Dragons. We're not your ancient heroes. We're a football team. Bottom of the league. We lost seven-nil today ... do you understand? I wish I had me clothes. I feel ridiculous like this.

Chief We understand.

Chris Thank heavens for that.

Chief Touch the ring once more.

Chris Yes. Sorry. Bye.

He touches the ring. Magically he now wears a sword, and a sorcery-type hero's costume

Chief This is more fitting.

Chris (*sarcastically*) Oh yes. Much better. I don't feel at all ridiculous now. You're not following me, are you? Watch my lips. The *Golden Dragon* is a pub. Pub.

They laugh happily

Chief You are wondering why we have summoned you after all this time.

Chris No, I'm not. I couldn't care less. I want to go home. Where is this anyway? Lewis's grotto?

Chief Come. We will explain all. Music.

Chris No, don't bother. Just ...

He is drowned out by the reprise of the anthem

Elflings   The seven Golden Dragons, golden, bold and strong
               Seven Golden Dragons, golden, bold and strong
               Seven Golden Dragons, seven Golden Dragons
               Our heroes, our legend, our song.

The Elflings carry him triumphantly as he protests, exasperated

Black-out

SCENE 6

A riverbank

Ben and his dad are sitting fishing

Ben Dad?

Dad Yeh.

Ben Do you remember you once said to me that I could always talk to you about anything?

Dad Yes.

Ben No matter what it was?

Dad Yes?

Ben Even if it was something that I didn't want to talk to mum about?

Dad (*nervously*) Yes. I remember.

Ben Even if it was, you know, embarrassing?

Dad (*more nervously*) Yes.

Ben Or if I was in any kind of trouble, how I shouldn't be afraid to tell you about it?

Dad Yes. Of course. (*He is very anxious now*)

Ben And do you remember you said if I had any questions or anything I didn't understand I should always ask you and not the other boys at school?

Dad Yes. That's right.

Long pause. Dad looks at Ben expectantly. Ben just fishes. Dad gets more and more exasperated and agitated. He is very fidgety and finally squeaks

Well what is it? What's the matter? What have you done?

Ben Well ... Dad ...

Dad Yes. Yes. What?

Ben Is it maggots or flies that are best for trout?

Dad Is that it?

Ben What?

Dad (*growing angry*) Is that your question?

Ben Yeh.

Dad, trying to restrain himself from hitting Ben, gets up

Where are you going?

Dad For a walk!

Dad exits

Ben They say fishing's supposed to make you relax.

Chris appears in hero costume

If that's our new team kit, forget it. I'm not running around in public dressed like that.

Chris Does it *look* like football kit?

Ben Well I thought you might have got us sponsored by that porno shop in the High Street. They have stuff like that.

Chris No, I've come to ... how do you know?

Ben Well it's called "Slap and Tickle". I thought it was a fishing shop.

Chris Well, listen. I need your help.

Ben Not another training session.

Chris No. This is a matter of life and death.

Ben Well what is it?

Chris You're going to find this hard to believe. After you left this morning these three Elflings came to the changing room looking for the Golden Dragons—not us but these other Golden Dragons but they didn't understand that. They live in the Blossom Marshes and they came to this world using this golden ring which helps them in times of trouble—I used it to get here actually. Only they're being attacked by these Orcs who work for Znakbar who wants the Ring of Magor—that's not this ring. It's this other ring which has enormous magic power and which they can never give up or their people will perish. They need our help. And I know this all sounds ridiculous but I couldn't do it alone so I've come to ask all the Golden Dragons to come back to the Blossom Marshes with me to help.

Ben OK. I'll just leave a note for me dad. (*Writes*) "Gone to the Blossom Marshes to help the Elflings and kill the Orcs. Back by tea time." These Elflings of yours?

Chris Yes.

Ben Are you sure they wouldn't be better off with the *Rose and Crown* team?

Chris No Ben. We're the Golden Dragons. It's part of the legend. It has to be us. Aren't you excited, Ben? This is better than fishing.

Song 5: This is Our Chance To Be Heroes

(*Singing*) This could be the only time
      In your dull existence here
      Someone needs your help and mine
      Why resist? Our duty's clear.

      No esteem, no thrills, no fun
      Each day after boring day
      Come with me and be someone
      Try to live another way.

      Don't ignore your destiny
      (You can be a hero)
      Leave all this and come with me
      (Not one of the zeroes)
      This is our chance to be the heroes of our lives.

Black-out

SCENE 7

A Church

The following is mimed to the singing of a choir. Rob, dressed as a choirboy is singing at a wedding. Choirboys on each side of him (or cardboard cutouts). Chris appears behind him and taps him on the shoulder. Rob carries on singing, motioning Chris to get lost. Chris is telling him the whole story. Rob is incredulous. Chris is insistent. Rob tries to sing on. Eventually Chris holds out the ring indicating that Rob should touch it if he doesn't believe him. Will Chris go away if Rob does so? Yes. So Rob touches the ring. Suddenly Rob is dressed very similarly to Chris. He is horrified and edges out of the church deeply embarrassed

Black-out

SCENE 8

A Clothes Shop

Gary and his little brother, Barry, are arguing with their mother

Gary Oh, God, this is really embarrassing. Mum, we're too old for you to come with us when we're buying clothes.

Barry Yeh.

Mum Oh yes, I know you two. If I left it to you you'd come back home dressed like a couple of punk rockers.

Gary I hope we don't meet anyone I know.

Barry Yeh.

Mum Well, I'm sorry if you're ashamed to be seen with me but as it's my money you're spending I'm going to make sure you're not wasting it.

Gary We're only buying jeans and shirts. How could we waste money on them?

Barry Yeh.

Mum I haven't forgotten those shirts you bought last summer. The price of them! And now you won't wear them.

Gary They're pink. No one's wearing pink shirts now. We'd get skitted if we went out wearing them.

Barry Yeh.

Mum I'm not arguing with you. Barry, these jeans. Go in that cubicle and try them on.

Barry But I want Levis.

Mum They're identical. No difference except the label and they're half the price. If you think I'm paying out hard-earned money just for a fancy label . . .

Barry But Mum . . .

Mum *Get in that cubicle and try them on!*

Barry goes in

Now what about you? Look at these. They're very reasonable. (*She holds up a pair of underpants*)

Gary (*very embarrassed*) Will you put them down! We came for shirts, not underwear.

Mum I know but they're in the sale and you won't find them cheaper anywhere else. (*She holds them in front of Gary to see the size*)

Gary snatches them away

Gary Will you stop it! People are looking.

Mum Let them look. They must be short of entertainment if they want to watch me buying underpants. (*She holds a pair up and shouts to onlookers*) What do you think? Would he look better in the blue or the white.

Gary cringes in embarrassment

Gary Can we go home now?

Mum What about your shirt?

Gary Forget it. I'll wear the pink one. Can we just *go*?!

Mum Barry's still trying on those jeans.
Gary Barry, will you hurry up?

Barry emerges from the cubicle in hero-type clothing. Mum and Gary are taken aback

Barry Do you like it? Great, isn't it?
Mum Barry Fazeley! What do you think you look like?
Gary Where did you find all that?
Barry It's Chris. In there. He wants to talk to you too.

Gary goes into the cubicle looking puzzled

Mum Now don't think I'm buying that 'cos I'm not. You look like something out of a comic.
Barry Mum, you don't understand. I'm a hero. I'm going with Chris to fight the Orcs.
Mum What have I told you about fighting in the street and gangs? Is that what this is, your uniform? And I've told Gary about hanging around with that Chris Norton. Just 'cos he's in the same football team, it doesn't mean he's got to to let him take over his life. He wanted to go training this afternoon after playing a match this morning. Football, football, football, that's all some lads think about. I wish he'd put as much effort into his schoolwork as he does into his football and his pop music.

Gary emerges in hero costume, followed by Chris

What are *you* doing in there? What's going on? Have you any idea what you all look like?
Gary Which do you think looks the best, the red headband or the yellow?
Mum Christopher Norton, this is one of your loony ideas, isn't it? (*She notices people are watching and shouts at them*) What are you looking at? My children have lost their minds and you think it's entertainment! Now both of you get back in the cubicle and get dressed properly and as for you Christopher Norton, when I see your mother . . .
Chris Mrs Fazeley.
Mum What?
Chris You see this ring? Well, I was wondering do you think it's real gold?
Mum Real gold! Where would you get a real gold . . .

She touches it to examine it, screams, and disappears

Gary Where's she gone?
Chris It's all right. I've just transported her to the shop next door.
Gary "Slap and Tickle"?
Chris Never mind her . . .

Song 5: (*reprise*) This Is Our Chance To Be Heroes

Parents, teachers, friends at school
Want you to be normal too
Uniforms, traditions, rules
All to stop you being you.

This could be the only time
In your dull existence here
Someone needs your help and mine
Why resist? Our duty's clear.

Grab this opportunity
(You can be a hero)
Be what you were meant to be
(Not one of the zeroes)
This is our chance to be the heroes of our lives.

Black-out

SCENE 9

Znakbar's Lair

Znakbar strides on stage, double-taking at a member of audience

Znakbar What are you looking at? Be careful lest you arouse the wrath of—
Znakbar! Where is the Elfling? Bring him in!

Porc enters very tentatively

Bring in the Elfling, I say!

Porc comes closer, very nervously

Let there be no more delay, lest you arouse the wrath of—Znakbar!

Snorc and Gorc hover in the background

The Elfling!
Porc Yes, master . . . er . . .
Znakbar Where is the disgusting furry creature?
Porc It escaped.

Pause. Znakbar stares menacingly

But we can get another. Or a few. Some spares. In case you feel like
torturing something. You know, like you do sometimes. Instead of
mutilating one of us, you could take an Elfling out of stock. Good idea,
isn't it?

Snorc and Gorc join Porc

It was Snorc who thought of it actually.
Znakbar ESCAPED!

The Orcs all begin to run away

STOP!

They stop

HERE!

They come to him and prostrate themselves

WHAT HAVE YOU DONE? (*He kicks Porc*)

Porc We have aroused the wrath of—Znakbar!

Orcs Znakbar!

Znakbar Go and throw yourselves into the dungeons—and torture each other a bit.

The Orcs exit

They're hopeless. They'll have to go. I think I'll take on a few school leavers on one of those schemes. Anybody interested? A year's training with the possibility of a permanent job at the end of it? Only one qualification required. You have to be thoroughly, scummily, scabbily, *evil*. Anybody out there got what it takes?

Song 6: Join My Team

Znakbar   Do you want to join my team?
Have some fun and gain esteem?
Be a good guy—be a fool
In the nineties *bad* is cool

(*Speaking*) Now let me see. What do I need? I'm looking for the dregs of society here.

Mugger from the park
Soccer fan or two
People who push past you in the dinner queue
Burglar in the dark
Gorilla from the zoo
Ask the maths department to supply a few.

Do you want to join my team?
Have some fun and gain esteem
Be a good guy—be a fool
In the nineties *bad* is cool.

Drunks who drive too fast
Tyrants, ticket touts
Mad axe killers, thugs, street corner layabouts
Gunmen from Belfast
Renegade boy scouts
Plane hijackers, terrorists and litter louts

Do you want to join my crew?
Could be tailor made for you
Golden opportunity
One day you could be like *me*!

Dentist on the job
Vandal in the street

Teenager who never keeps his bedroom neat
Hit man for the mob
Liar or a cheat
People who leave chewing gum stuck to your seat

Bully in the yard
Psycho out on bail
People who send advertising through the mail
Schoolboy acting hard
Scotsman on the ale
Anyone at all who works for British Rail.

Do you want to join my team?
Have some fun and gain esteem
Be a good guy—be a fool
In the nineties *bad* is cool.

Do you want to join my crew?
Could be tailor made for you
Golden opportunity
One day you could be like *me*!

Black-out

SCENE 10

An aeroplane
Two pilots on the flight deck. Pilot 2 is very nervous and frantically switches,
checks dials

Pilot 1 (*picking up the microphone*) Good afternoon, ladies and gentlemen.
This is your captain speaking. On behalf of Impact Airways I would like
to welcome you aboard. We hope you enjoy the flight. We are now flying
at a height of (*he consults the dial*) thirty feet . . .

He taps dial and draws attention of other pilot to it. Pilot 2 fiddles with it
nervously, looks out of the window, sees it is thirty feet and grabs control
column. Pulls it back sharply. They lean back at dangerous angle.

. . . and at a speed of six hundred m.p.h. Below us you can see the Atlantic
Ocean and we will be arriving in New York in about six hours.

Pilot 2 waves a clipboard in Pilot 1's face

Below us you can see the English Channel, the weather is favourable and
we will be arriving in Malaga in about three hours. (*He puts down the*
microphone) Take over, Mike. I just want to stretch my legs.
Pilot 2 Me? Take over? Are you sure that's wise?
Pilot 1 Why not? You're a qualified, experienced pilot, aren't you?
Pilot 2 Yes, but you know what happened last time.

Pilot 1 That could happen to anyone.

Pilot 2 That's not what they said at the inquest.

Pilot 1 Look. We are flying straight and level. The automatic pilot is in operation. What can go wrong?

Pilot 2 What can go wrong? What can go wrong. Have you never heard of metal fatigue? Instrument failure? Freak storms? Fuel leaks? Engines catching fire? Bombs? Hijacks? Crazed terrorists with machine guns? Hundreds of tons of metal hurtling through the air, thousands of feet above the Bay of Biscay and all controlled by a bunch of electronic gadgets no one understands—what's that dial? That one there. I never know what that is. You don't know either, do you?

Pilot 1 Well . . .

Pilot 2 Nobody knows. And you ask me what can go wrong. *A million things can go wrong!* Human beings were never meant to fly. It's against nature and one day we'll pay for it, mark my words, we'll pay for it. (*He breaks down in floods of hysterical tears*)

Pilot 1 Listen, Mike. The aircraft was completely overhauled only last week. It's in A1 condition.

Pilot 2 sobs

The weather forecast is for clear skies all day.

Pilot 2 sniffs

Sniffer dogs examined the plane for explosives just before we took off.

Pilot 2 is calmer

And airport security has been doubled since that latest outbreak of trouble in the Middle East.

Pilot 2 has almost recovered

That's better. Now you just keep an eye on things for a few minutes while I go back into the cabin and don't worry. Everything will be fine. (*He turns to go*)

Chris enters behind them. He freezes, horrified

Pilot 2 (*not seeing Chris*) Yes. I'm OK now. Sorry about that. I've been a little on edge lately.

Chris Excuse me. Sorry to bother you. Is this flight B-seven-nine-one-oh to Malaga?

Pilot 2 (*he turns, sees Chris, shrieks*) Aaaagh! Oh no! (*He falls on the control column*)

The plane nosedives. They all tilt forward. Pilot 1 rights the plane

Don't shoot. Don't shoot. Whatever you do, don't shoot. Have you any idea what happens if a bullet goes through one of these windows? We all get sucked out through the hole! What do you want? What do you want? Anything. *Just don't shoot!*

Chris I'm looking for Matt.

Pilot 2 Matt? Matt! (*Grabbing maps*) Where is it? Matt. Matt. Don't worry. I'll find it. Is it near Beirut? I don't know if we've got enough fuel.

Chris It's not a place. I'm looking for Matthew Kingswood. He's supposed to be on this flight.

Pilot 2 Oh! A hostage? A vendetta? Well, if he's out there, you can have him. Help yourself. My saf . . . the safety of the other passengers comes first. Here . . . I'll get him up here. (*Picking up the microphone*) This is your pilot speaking. There is no need to panic. Everything is fine. Don't worry. The stewardesses are trained to deal with every kind of emergency. Will Mr Matthew Kingswood please come forward to the flight deck. It's quite safe. There is no danger. This is not a trick. Mr Matthew Kingswood to the flight deck please. (*He puts the microphone down, then has an afterthought and picks it up again*) Come alone and unarmed.

Pilot 1 That's an interesting uniform. Middle East Liberation Front?

Chris No. I'm a Golden Dragon.

Pilot 1 Oh. Are you on the left or the right?

Chris Depends where you're coming from.

Pilot 1 Oh yeh. Of course. Where you're coming from. Yes. Well I have a great deal of sympathy for groups like yours struggling away to make the world a better place for . . . for . . . er . . .

Chris Elflings.

Pilot 2 (*to Pilot 1*) I knew it. Headcase. They're the worst. He could do anything . . . run amok any minute . . . humour him.

Matt enters

Matt Excuse me. Did you want to see me? Chris! What are you doing here?

Chris talks to Matt as:

Pilot 2 (*to Pilot 1*) It's a trick. They're a team working together. It's no good. We'll have to overpower them.

Pilot 1 (*to Pilot 2*) Look. I'm not sure. The regulations recommend.

Pilot 2 (*to Pilot 1*) Don't quote the regulations at me. This is an emergency. Pretend we're going along with them until I give you the signal.

Pilot 1 But . . .

Chris bursts into song

Song 5 (*reprise*): This Is Our Chance To Be Heroes

Chris (*singing*) No esteem, no thrills, no fun
Each day after boring day
Come with me and be someone
Try to live another way.

Matt is not convinced at first. Pilot 2 joins in the song and encourages Pilot 1 to do the same. There is a dance routine during which Pilot 2 tries to sneak up on and overpower Chris and Matt

Grab this opportunity
(You can be a hero)

Be what you were meant to be
(Not one of the zeroes)
This is our chance to be the heroes of our lives.

Don't ignore the summons when
You can be a hero
It's a chance won't come again
Not one of the zeroes
This is our chance to be the heroes of our lives.

Don't ignore the summons when
You can be a hero
It's a chance won't come again
Not one of the zeroes
This is our chance to be the heroes of our lives.

Chris and Matt disappear by touching the ring

The Pilots sing on and finish the song

The plane starts nose-diving. The Pilots fight to regain control. They do so. They wipe their brows and relax

A real hijacker enters

Hijacker Listen carefully. I want you to take this plane to Cuba.

The Pilots burst into tears

Black-out

SCENE 11

A stand at a football match

A crowd watching a match. Steve is in the middle of them. Chris appears, pushing through the crowd

Steve Hi, Chris. What are you doing? What's that you're wearing?
Chris (*watching the match*) What's the score?
Steve One-nil to them. You look amazing. What is it?
Chris (*watching the match*) Look at that. Half a million quid and he misses a sitter like that!
Steve Chris! What is going on? You look ready for a fancy dress party not a football match.

Chris and crowd react to a near-missed shot

Is that real gold round your neck? And that ring is amazing. Let's have a look.

Chris holds the ring up but still watches the match intently

Is there some kind of writing on it? (*He touches it*)

The crowd disappears

Black-out

SCENE 12

The Elfling Camp

Chris and Steve stand as at end of Scene 11 but are now surrounded by other Golden Dragons and Elflings

Chris Oh! You could have waited till half-time!

Steve What's happened? Where are we? What's going on?

The other six begin to sing, dressing Steve in heroic costume as they do so

Song 5 (*reprise*): **This Is Our Chance To Be Heroes**

> This could be the only time
> In your dull existence here
> Someone needs your help and mine
> Why resist? Our duty's clear
>
> Parents, teachers, friends at school
> Want you to be normal too
> Uniforms, traditions, rules
> All to stop you being you
>
> Grab this opportunity
> (You can be a hero)
> Be what you were meant to be
> (Not one of the zeroes)
> This is our chance to be the heroes of our lives
>
> Don't ignore the summons when
> You can be a hero
> It's a chance won't come again
> Not one of the zeroes
> This is our chance to be the heroes of our lives

Chief The Seven Golden Dragons! Now all will be well. How can we thank you? You have saved us all.

Rob I think the first thing we should do is to decide a plan so that the next time these Orcs attack we're ready for them.

Barry Yeh!

Gary Shut up, Barry.

Grimbo If you could drive the Orcs away our life here in the Blossom Marshes would be bliss.

Ben Erm ... these Orcs. What are they like exactly?

Grimbo Hideously ugly.

Gazebo With the strength of giants.

Snorbo Cruel.

Garbo Vicious.

Limbo We do not like them.

Ben How many of them are there?

Grimbo There are many.

Gazebo An army of them.

Snorbo And then there is their Lord.

Garbo Znakbar.

Elflings Znakbar!

Chief But now with the Golden Dragons to defend us all will be well. (*He is tearful*) Excuse me. After so many hundreds of years, that you should return to save us, my heart is overcome with joy.

Rob I think we should divide everyone into teams to defend the different approaches to the village. We do not know where the Orcs will attack next.

Barry Yeh.

Gary Shut up, Barry.

Matt Chief, if you could divide your people into groups each of us could plan how best to defend one area.

Chief My people? I do not understand.

Grimbo You want *us* to fight?

Snorbo You do not understand. We are a peaceful people.

Limbo That is why we sent for you.

Ben You mean you want *us* to fight the Orcs?

Steve Alone?

Chief Yes. You are the Golden Dragons.

The seven look nervously at each other

Matt What is it, exactly, that the Orcs want from you?

Chief The Ring of Magor! The ancient treasure of our people.

Steve Perhaps if you gave it to them they would leave you in peace.

Chief We cannot.

Grimbo It has great power.

Trumbo It is the soul of our race.

Limbo It is more precious to us than life itself.

Chief And we don't know where it is.

Chris Well I'm afraid the seven of us are not enough to fight off these Orcs.

Chief I see. Then my people must perish.

Gary No. You must act. You must fight. You must stick up for yourselves.

Barry Yeh.

Other 6 Shut up, Barry!

Song 7: Stand Up For Yourselves

Chris   Znakbar
                    Won't leave you alone and there's
                    One thing
                    You'd be fools to deny
                    You can't
                    Survive on your own unless

You can look him in the eye

Chorus

Dragons   Stand up
                  Stand up and be counted
                  Stand up stand up for your rights
                  It's time to stand up for yourselves
                  It's time to stand up for yourselves
                  Stand up to them, stand and fight

Chris   Lie down
                  And they'll walk all over you
                  Step back
                  And they'll brush you aside
                  Stand firm
                  It's time to say, "no", for you
                  Have to resist—or die

Chorus

Dragons   Stand up
                  Stand up and be counted
                  Stand up stand up for your rights
                  It's time to stand up for yourselves
                  It's time to stand up for yourselves
                  Stand up to them, stand and fight

Repeat second verse and chorus

Chris Now Elflings, are you with us?
Elflings (*roused*) Yes!
Chris Are you going to give in to Znakbar?
Elflings No!
Chris Are you ready to fight?
Elflings Yes!

Znakbar and the Orcs enter unseen by Chris

Chris All for one and one for all!
Elflings No!

Elflings begin to flee but more Orcs appear at exits and stop them

Znakbar Ha, ha, ha! Surely you do not expect these Elflings to fight. They are the feeblest of creatures, born for slavery. And they shall be my slaves as soon as they tell me how I can obtain the Ring of Magor.
Chris You must be Znakbar. How do you do?

They shake hands

I'm Chris. This is Steve ... Ben ...

In the midst of the hand shaking Znakbar screams

Znakbar So, Elflings! You think these Golden Dragons will save you. How dare you challenge the might of Znakbar!

Orcs Znakbar!

Znakbar Kill two ... no, three of them, immediately.

Chris No!

Znakbar Look. This is none of your business. No one's going to miss a few Elflings. Orcs!

Orcs grab three Elflings

Chris Release them. Release them at once or take the consequences.

Znakbar Ha, ha, ha, ha! Kill them!

The Orcs draw weapons. The Golden Dragons attack the Orcs. They do not do very well

Matt Elflings! You must act now! Help us!

Znakbar Ha, ha, ha, ha!

Gary Fight! You must fight or perish for ever! Fight with us!

Barry is swung round by his feet by an Orc

Barry Yeh!

The Elflings join in fighting. Battle. Znakbar and the Orcs are defeated. The Elflings and the Golden Dragons begin to leave, congratulating themselves

Znakbar (*from the floor*) Come back! That wasn't fair! We weren't ready!

The Elflings and the Golden Dragons start to come back

Znakbar No! No! Only kidding. Fair fight! No one has ever accused me of being a bad loser.

The Elflings and the Golden Dragons go, jeering. When they have gone ...

I'm not a bad loser! I'm not a loser at all! I don't give up that easily! I'm warning you! You won't get away with this. From now on I'm going to get nasty! Get up, you Orcs. Back to the Swamp Palace. This is only a temporary setback. A little re-training may be necessary but then we will return!

Song 8: We'll Be Back

Znakbar
You think that I'm down
While you go for a snack
I'll get off the ground
And I will be back

Go and have a break
Get a cup of tea
But don't imagine that
You've seen the back of me

Znakbar
and Orcs
Back
We'll be back, you haven't satisfied us

Back!
We'll be back to take what you've denied us
Back!
We'll be back to pull the legs off spiders
Back!
Yes, we'll be back!

Back!
We'll make you very sorry you defied us
Back!
With all the evil spawn of hell beside us
Back!
You should *see* us after three dry ciders!
Back!
Yes, we'll be back!

Znakbar   Go and have a break
Get a cup of tea
But don't imagine that
Don't imagine that
Don't imagine that
You've seen the last of me!

Black-out

INTERVAL

ACT II

SCENE 1

The Swamp Palace

Znakbar appears, hauling on a rope with great difficulty. With a great struggle he manages to reach centre stage fighting all the way

Znakbar This is ridiculous! I'm supposed to be in charge round here. I shouldn't have to do this. Orcs! Orcs! Get in here—now!

The Orcs enter. They watch Znakbar's struggles

Porc What are you doing, O mighty one?
Snorc Is it aerobics?
Znakbar (*struggling*) No. I'm ... It's ...
Gorc You know what your problem is there, don't you?
Znakbar I ... no ... will you ...
Gorc Your grip's all wrong.

Znakbar falls and is being dragged towards the wings

Znakbar Will you help me with this!

The Orcs leap into action and take over the rope. Znakbar gets up and dusts himself down

Porc What is it?
Znakbar A Glinch.

The Orcs all shriek and drop the rope. Znakbar chases after it and struggles back on with it to the centre of the stage

Znakbar Get hold of this thing!

The Orcs do so very nervously

Znakbar What's the matter with you? You're a disgrace to the noble order of Orcs. What are you?
Orcs A disgrace to the noble order of Orcs, O mighty Znakbar.
Gorc Znakbar!
Torc Pardon me, your gracious magnificence, but did you say there is a Glinch at the end of this rope?
Znakbar Yes, of course.
Torc A *live* Glinch?
Znakbar Yes. Yes. What's the matter?

Skworc When you say a Glinch, do you mean the most vicious and revolting creature in the whole of the black regions of creation, that sort of Glinch?

Znakbar Yes. What other sort of Glinch is there? The common Glinch — the hideous spawn of the foulest swamps, the most utterly degraded monster in the universe.

Forc On the end of this rope?

Znakbar How many times? Yes!

Torc How old is it?

Znakbar How do I know?

Snorc Is it a baby one?

Gorc All cute and cuddly?

Znakbar No! It is mean and vicious, a full-sized adult Glinch!

Porc Pardon me, O mighty one, but could I ask ...

Znakbar No more questions! You may see it for yourselves. Get it in here.

Orcs In here?

Znakbar Yes. Right now.

The Orcs haul in the Glinch. It is huge and ugly with a large mouth and a label tied round its neck

Tie it to that pillar.

The Orcs do so

The man in the pet shop said there were full instructions for looking after it. Ah, yes, look. (*To Porc*) Fetch me that label.

Porc (*to Snorc*) Fetch the label.

Snorc (*to Gorc*) Fetch the label.

Gorc (*to Znakbar*) Fetch the label.

Znakbar What? (*Hitting Gorc*) Get it!

Gorc whimpers (like Stan Laurel) and very nervously approaches the Glinch. It moves and he runs away

Gorc I can't get it! It'll eat me!

Znakbar Those are important instructions. If we don't look after it properly, it might start to fret.

Torc (*sympathetically*) Aaah.

The Glinch starts to fret. The Orcs scream

Znakbar Oh, you are *pathetic*! I'll get it myself.

He does so. The Glinch goes for him. He gets the label, the Orcs make a feeble show of helping him

Znakbar (*reading the label*) Ah, I thought so. Look at this.

The Orcs gather round to look, bumping into Znakbar. He moves them away

It says here that if this Glinch is not fed at least three times a day it could become very aggressive.

The Glinch starts to become aggressive

Go and fetch some slaves.

The Orcs exit

Don't worry, Glinchy. Supper's on the way. Now let me see. What can we offer you?

He goes to the blackboard and heads it "Menu". The Orcs bring in slaves

You lot! What are your names?

Slaves (*variously*)   Patrick.
                           Kevin.
                           Roland.
                           Richard.
                           Keith.
                           Gordon.
                           Peter.
                           Stewart.
                           Sean.

Znakbar Perfect! Ha, ha, ha! You stand here, then you . . . (*He re-arranges them and then scribbles on the blackboard*) OK. OK. Are you ready, Glinch?

The Glinch roars

OK. OK. He, he, he. First course.

He grabs Sean and puts some lettuce on his head

Sean cocktail.

He roars with laughter, signalling to the Orcs who feed Sean to the Glinch. Znakbar laughs madly

Did you like that? Now for the entree, sir. This time you get a choice.

He brings Keith, Stewart and Peter forward

You can have . . . ha ha ha . . . listen, listen, you can have . . . Roast Keith . . . ha ha ha . . . or . . . no, this is good . . . listen . . . Roast Keith or Irish Stew . . . or . . . or . . .

Peter (*falling to his knees*) No. No. Please, O mighty one, spare me. I don't want to be a lunch's Glinch, I mean a Glinch's lunch. I don't want to die. I'm frightened. I can't bear to think of those teeth crunching my bones. No. No. Please no. Spare me. Spare me. No. No. No. No. No. (*He is hysterical. He subsides*)

Znakbar . . . or a little ham?

The Glinch growls

The Roast Keith? An excellent choice, sir, if I may say so.

He puts an apple in Keith's mouth and Keith is fed screaming to the Glinch

Skworc Master . . . tee hee . . . master?

Znakbar What is it?

Skworc Do you think he would like a drink? 'Cos we could give him . . . ha ha ha ha . . .

He goes over to Gordon and points

We could give him Gordon's chin.

Znakbar and the Orcs fall about laughing

Porc And master, master, look.

He hands a tub of butter to Roland

You forgot . . . ha ha ha . . . look. Roland—Butter.

They collapse. The Glinch growls

Znakbar Oh look. He's ready for the sweet course. (*He looks at the remaining slaves*) Well, what have we got left? Assorted fruits? No, no, no. Oh no . . . ha ha ha . . . this is brilliant . . . ha ha ha . . . I'm a scream sometimes . . . look . . . look.

He pulls Richard out of line, gets a paintbrush and paint and covers him in dots

Spotted Dick!

Znakbar and the Orcs roll on the floor, banging their heels, hysterically. Finally Znakbar signals and Dick is fed to the Glinch, screaming horribly. Glinch burps

That seems to have satisfied him. Take these to the kitchen and put them on a low light.

The Orcs take some of the surviving slaves, and they exit

Oh, I haven't had so much fun since granny fell in the septic tank. It's such a tonic, laughter, don't you think? Mummy always used to say I'd missed my vocation. I should have been a schoolteacher. I do enjoy it so when they scream. In my opinion, over the years, the appeal of cruelty has been much underrated.

Znakbar approaches a remaining slave and slips a cord around his neck, tightening it

Song 9: It's A Scream

Though I like the strangled gurgle as I tighten the garotte
And the muffled crack of snapping bones I do enjoy a lot

He jerks a slave's head sharply around. There is a crack. The slave falls dead

The only sound that moves me like a sweet orchestral theme
Must be a scream.

He approaches the slaves, hitting them with a stick to produce the screams in the chorus

Chorus

Slaves	Aaagh!
Znakbar	A cry of pain can have for me
Slaves	Aaagh!
Znakbar	The beauty of a symphony
Slaves	Aaagh!
Znakbar	Though it may seem extreme
	I think
	It's a scream

He approaches the slaves with a knife

> To feel a blade rip through the skin is to feel sweet ecstasy
> A victim's face contort with fear and pain's a joy to see
> But for sheer sensual pleasure of the like of which you'd
> dream
> Give me a scream

Chorus

Znakbar stabs slaves. The Glinch starts to become restless

Znakbar (*speaking*) Don't you agree with me, Glinchy?
Glinch (*speaking*) I know where you're coming from, man.

> Despite the satisfying crunch as I bite off each one's head
> And though I thrill to taste their blood and see it running
> red
> It adds a further piquancy, a succulence supreme
> To hear them scream.

Chorus

*Znakbar lights a match which he uses on the slaves to produce a chorus of
screams but on the last he burns himself. Znakbar now sings verse 1 and Glinch
sings verse 3 at the same time. Then both sing a final chorus, Znakbar running
around madly and doing the screams himself hysterically*

Black-out

SCENE 2

Elfling camp

Feasting and celebrations are going on

Chief Now, Elflings, in honour of our guests we must all sing the Elfling
celebration anthem.

Elflings cheer

Grimbo This is the ancient song of our people—handed down over the
centuries—always by word of mouth. It has never been written down. Are
we ready Elflings?

Elflings Yes.

Grimbo sounds a note. The Elflings then sing an improvised song of meaning-less gibberish and horrible discords. It is vaguely reminiscent of a sixties flower power song

Song 10: Celebration Anthem

The song ends

Steve Handed down by word of mouth?
Ben Never written down?
Chief Forgive me. The celebration anthem always makes me weep. It is so moving.
Chris Thank you all, Elflings, for your hospitality but now it is time for us to return.
Chief (*shocked*) Return?
Grimbo Leave us?
Rob Yes, we're playing the *Farmers Arms* in the Mothercare Cup tomorrow.
Chris Yes, our job here is done.
Chief But ... but ... Znakbar and the Orcs ... they are sure to return.

The Elflings look around nervously

Steve You have defeated them once. You can do it again.
Snorbo By ourselves?
Limbo All alone?
Obo Without any help?
Steve We've taught you all we know.
Ben Putting the boot in.
Ron Head butting.
Matt Eye gouging.
Gary Knee-capping.
Rob Bricking the away supporters ... oh no ... sorry.
Chief You have taught us how to fight but you have not taught us how to be brave. You are our courage and if you leave us you take our courage with you.
Matt But we can't stay here for ever.
Garbo Please stay. It is not our fault. When the goblins stole from us the Silver Sword of Sagar, they took with it the strength of our people.
Chris What is this Silver Sword of Sagar?
Chief Well it's a sword, made of silver ... from Sagar.
Chris Yes, I see.
Chief Legend has it that only if we recover the sword will the Elflings regain the spirit of our warrior ancestors, proud defenders of the poor and weak.
Matt Do you know where the sword is?
Grimbo It is said that the goblins took it to the Mountain of Terror.
Rob Mountain of Terror?
Snorbo Yes, it lies beyond the Swamp of Doom.
Limbo Through the Forest of Nightmares.

Trumbo Across the Black Valley of the Night Creatures.
Barry Oh yeh, I know it. It's right next to Sainsbury's.
Other 6 Shut up, Barry.
Chief If we had the silver sword we could fight Znakbar and defeat his Orcs.
Ben Chris, don't even think about it.   .
Matt Think about what?
Chris Then there is only one thing to do.
Ben He thought about it.
Rob Oh no.
Steve You don't want us to go to the Mountain of Terrors?
Gary Through the Forest of Nightmares?
Rob Across the Black Valley of the Night Creatures?
Barry (*whispering*) Right next to Sainsbury's.

The other six hit him

Garbo Erm . . .
Matt What?
Garbo You forgot the Swamp of Doom.
Ben You see, Chris, you forgot the Swamp of Doom. I mean that clinches it
for me. Mountain of Terrors—well OK. Forest of Nightmares—no
sweat. Black Valley of the Night Creatures—I can handle it. But there is
no way, *no way*, I am going anywhere near . . . er . . .
Barry Sainsbury's.
Ben Sainsbury's . . . no . . . the . . . what was it?
Garbo The Swamp of Doom.
Ben Yeh, Swamp of Doom.
Chris Ben, we cannot abandon these Elflings to the revenge of Znakbar.
Barry Znakbar!
Other 6 Shut up, Barry.
Ben Well, no, I suppose not *abandon* them.
Chris And we cannot remain here indefinitely.
Barry Indefinitely not.

Barry is thumped

Chris So we have no alternative. We must bring back the Silver Sword of
Sagar from the Mountain of Terror.
Ben But, Chris, what if we get grabbed by the goblins?
Chris (*after a long pause*) We must take that chance. Are we all agreed?
Barry Yes!
Chris Good.
Other 5 Shut up, Barry!
Chris We will leave at once.
Chief There will be great danger.
Chris How do we find this Mountain of Terror?
Chief I fear the way has been long forgotten by my people.
Ben Oh well, that's that then, isn't it? Nice try, Chris, but if they don't know
where it is, we could set off in completely the wrong direction. I'm sorry,
but it is really . . .

Chief There is one who knows.
Ben There would be.
Chief You must ask Wakelam, the wise old man. He will tell you all you need.
Ben That's all we need.
Chris And where can we find Wakelam, the wise old man?
Rob In the Castle of Destruction?
Matt Beyond the Desert of Blood?
Steve Deep in the Pit of Demons?
Barry Safeways?
Chief Shut up Barry. (*He hits Barry*) Wakelam, the wise old man, dwells beyond the River of Tranquility.
Steve Tranquility?
Ben I like it.
Chief It is a short journey. Take the western path and in six hours you will reach Wakelam's cave.
Rob Well, that sounds fairly straightforward at least.
Chris Let's not waste any more time. Are we all ready?

The others nod

Chief One word of warning. The cave of Wakelam, the wise old man ... well, there may be danger.
Ben The River of Tranquility is full of piranha fish?
Chief No. No. You should be quite safe as long as you take care ...

Song 11: Watch Your Step

(*Singing*)   Watch your step
                       Take a look over your shoulder
                       Keep alert keep alive
                       Don't relax
                       If you want to get older
                       And there's a very good chance
                       That you'll survive.

Rainbo   There's a seven-headed dragon
                       Fourteen kinds of deadly snake
                       There's a goblin that jumps at you
                       From a tree
                       There are vampire bats and banshees
                       There's a slime beast in the lake
                       But no danger if you proceed
                       Cautiously

Elflings   Watch your step
                       Take a look over your shoulder
                       Keep alert keep alive
                       Don't relax
                       If you want to get older
                       And there's a very good chance

That you'll survive

Chief
There's a demon lies in wait to
Sink its teeth into your throat
There's a monster wants to rip you limb from limb
Avoid them and the chances
Of disaster are remote
But just in case who is your
Next of kin?

Elflings
Watch your step
Take a look over your shoulder
Keep alert keep alive
Don't relax
If you want to get older
And there's a very good chance
That you'll survive

Rainbo
Don't go near the giant scorpions
For their poison there's no cure
Mutant zombies there will treat you
As a snack
But though it might be dangerous
Stick together and I'm sure
That maybe one or two of you
Will get back

Chief
Elflings *(together)*
Watch your step
Take a look over your shoulder
Keep alert keep alive
Don't relax
If you want to get older
And there's a very good chance
That you'll survive

Watch your step
Take a look over your shoulder
Keep alert keep alive
Don't relax
If you want to get older
And there's a very good chance
That you'll survive

Chris OK. Let's go.
Chief Goodbye. Good luck.
Elflings You'll need it.

The Golden Dragons march on the spot in line side-by-side facing the front

The Elflings fade into the background, waving

Black-out

SCENE 3

The Cave of Wakelam

*Rob, Steve, Ben, Barry, Chris, Matt and Gary are striding purposefully,
determined. It grows darker. A wind starts to howl. They slow a little. Owls
hoot. It grows darker still. Wolves howl. They slow to a crawl, looking nervous*

Rob Where are we now?
Steve (*consulting the map*) I think this is the Wolf Wood.
Ben Wolf Wood? Why's it called that?
Barry Because it's full of hedgehogs.

Howls

Chris I think we had better quicken our pace.

Howl behind them. They all look over their shoulders

All Wolves! Run!

*They run on the spot. Barry slowly falls behind. They urge him on. He catches
up. They run on*

Chris Stream!

They all leap across and run on

Chris Stream!

They leap, then run

Chris Stream!

They leap, fall and there is a splash. They clamber out. Howls. They run on

Barry You'd better watch out.
Others Shut up, Barry.
Barry I just thought I'd warn you about ...
Others Shut up, Barry.

The six fall down. Barry remains upright

Barry ... that low branch.

As they recover they hear a loud echoey voice over the speakers

Wakelam (*off*) Strangers, what seek ye with shouts in my silence?
                    Why in this Wolf Wood westerly wander?
Ben Oh no! What's that?
Chris It must be Wakelam, the wise old man.
Rob I *hope* it's Wakelam, the wise old man.
Wakelam (*off*) Hence from my home, happy here as a hermit
                    Leave me alone with my love of my loneliness.
Chris Are you ... is it Mr Wakelam?
Wakelam (*off*) Annoy me not with the name I was known by!
                    Close in my cave comes no one to call me.

Chris Er . . . Mr Wakelam, could we have a word with you, please?

Wakelam enters carrying a candle. He is at least three hundred years old but looks older

Wakelam Mist in my memory, full moon at midnight.

The six all look at each other in confusion

Chris Er . . . yes . . . Mr Wakelam . . . Benbo, the chief of the Elflings, told us you could help us.

Wakelam Fiery and flaming, full in the firmament.

Chris Yes, it is a lovely evening, isn't it?

Ben He's a loony. Let's get out of here.

Chris We can't. He's the only one who knows how to get to the sword.

Steve I'll get through to him. Listen—we want to find the Silver Sword of Sagar. Can you tell me where it is?

Wakelam Darkling at dewfall, deep in the dim light.

Rob Are you sure this is Wakelam, the wise old man?

Gary More like Wakelam, the silly old coot.

Barry Look out. (*To Wakelam*) Warm in your welcome, white-haired with
    wisdom
    Gladly we greet you, grim Golden Dragons
    Seeking a sword for assistance we sue.

Wakelam glares at Barry and gives in

Wakelam Oh really. Which sword is that then?

Rob (*to Gary*) Sometimes that brother of yours gets right up my nose.

Barry It's the Silver Sword of Sagar. We want to return it to the Elflings so that they can fight the evil Znakbar.

Wakelam We will find what you seek in the Ancient Book of Scrodor. I will fetch it. Tell your men to sit down. They must rest. They have a long journey ahead of them.

He exits

Barry Sit down, men. You must rest. You have a long journey . . .

The other six batter Barry

Wakelam returns with a dusty book. He opens it and flips through the pages for a long time then stops, frowns, looks up

Chris Well?

Wakelam (*puzzled*) What was it you wanted to know?

Rob The Silver Sword of Sagar.

Wakelam Oh yes. It's all in here, you know. (*Flipping pages*) All in here. (*He flips pages, stops and reads*)

Rob Have you found it?

Wakelam What? Oh sorry. Very good article on propagating tomatoes.

Chris Please. The Silver Sword of Sagar.

Wakelam Yes. Yes. You're so impatient. This book is full of wonders. The Silver Sword. The Silver Sword. Let me see . . . (*searching through*) . . . Ah.

Here. (*Mumbling*) "Silver Sword ... Sagar ... all the secrets of this legendary weapon are inscribed within the Ancient Scroll of Torpor." Of course. There you are.

He smiles at them. They look blank

Chris I'm sorry. I don't understand. Where is it?
Wakelam Where's what?
Rob The Silver Sword of flaming Sagar!
Wakelam I will consult the Ancient Book of Scrodor.

He starts to flip through the book again. The Golden Dragons look exasperated

Barry No. No. No. The Ancient Scroll of Torpor.
Wakelam (*looking up*) The Ancient Scroll of Torpor?
Barry Yes. Do you have a copy?
Wakelam No.
Barry Oh!
Wakelam I have the *original*!

He exits, returns, takes the book, exits, returns and approaches Barry, with a puzzled expression. Before he can speak Barry speaks

Barry The Ancient Scroll of Torpor.
Wakelam Excellent idea!

He exits and returns with a scroll

Here it is.
Rob (*taking the scroll*) Good. (*He lets go of one end and the scroll unrolls across the stage it is very long*)
Wakelam Take care! The scroll is over nine hundred years old.
Rob Sorry. Sorry. (*He tries to roll it up, creasing and tearing it in the process*)
Chris The Silver Sword of Sagar?
Barry Look. I saw it. Here. Look.
Chris "The Silver Sword of Sagar, according to legend, was hidden by the goblins in the caves of the Mountain of Terror."
Rob We already knew that. How do we get there?
Chris Here. Look. The goblin chief, Zoogoo ...
Ben (*in disbelief*) Zoogoo??
Chris Yeh. "The goblin chief, Zoogoo, ordered that a single map should be made of the precise location of the sword. It is said that the map was sealed with other secret goblin writings in the Ancient Chest of Olandia.
Wakelam I thought so. The Ancient Chest of Olandia.
Rob Where do we find that?
Wakelam It will not be easy.
Rob Where is it?
Wakelam Well, I think I saw it in the parlour last week but it could be in the lumber-room.

He stands smiling at them

Chris Could we look in it?
Wakelam Look in what?
Rob The Ancient Chest of Olandia!!!!!
Wakelam Oh yes. Wait please.

He exits and comes back

Rob hands him the scroll

He exits and comes back looking puzzled.

All The Ancient Chest of Olandia!

He exits and returns pulling an apparently very heavy chest, puffing and panting

Wakelam The Ancient Chest of Olandia.

Chris and Rob open it, searching through papers and removing various extraordinary items. Finally . . .

Rob Look. Look. The map. This is it. This is it. Look! Here's where we are. Look it's marked. The Cave of Wakelam, the dozy old twit.
Chris Wise old man.
Rob (*peering at the map*) Oh yeh. To reach the Mountain of Terror we take this road to the west, across here, then turn to the north and through this pass . . .
Barry Change at Oxford Circus.
Wakelam Shut up, Barry.
Chris Thank you, old man. With this we can find the sword and save the Elflings.

He hands the map to Rob who peers at it

Farewell!
Wakelam Farewell!

Rob consults the map and points to the back of the stage

The seven exit at the back

Wakelam goes to the chest and pulls it offstage with great difficulty, muttering and complaining. He then returns to pick up the papers etc, moaning all the time

The seven reappear, gesticulating and arguing

They snatch the map from each other. Barry finally turns it the right way up. and they stride on the spot in a line as before, waving to Wakelam

Wakelam exits, waving

Song 12: This Will Be Our Quest

Devils, demons, death and darkness
Put our courage to the test
To seek the Silver Sword of Sagar

This will be our quest

Light the lamp of liberation
Let it shine from east to west
Dedicated to our duty
This will be our quest

Force to flight the foes of freedom
We won't leave it to the rest
Striving, struggling, seeking, searching
This will be our quest

Devils, demons, death and darkness
Put our courage to the test
To seek the Silver Sword of Sagar
This will be our quest.

Black-out

SCENE 4

The Quest

Rob, Steve, Matt, Gary, Ben, Barry and Chris enter. Steve has the map and stops them

Steve Hold it. Wait. Be careful. Look what it says here. "Here lies danger."
    And then there's something in smaller print. I can't see it properly.
Matt Here. (*He lights a match and holds it for Steve*)
Steve That's better. "The home of Bacillus".
Matt What's a bacillus?

Bacillus enters behind them

Bacillus I am Bacillus!

They turn to see a fearsome creature. It has the body of a man but the head of a bull with huge horns. Matt holds the match too near the map which goes up in flames and is destroyed

Chris Ah yes. How do you do?

He approaches Bacillus with a hand outstretched. Bacillus roars, lowers his head and charges. They scatter. He stands with his back to the audience. The seven face him

No, I don't think you understand. We do not wish to fight. We are on our way to the Mountain of Terror—just passing through as it were. We won't trouble you any further.

They go to pass Bacillus but he stands in their way

Bacillus You may pass . . .

Chris Thank you so much.

They move but Bacillus still blocks their way

Bacillus You may pass when you pay my price!
Chris Price? What price?
Bacillus A feast.
Chris A feast? Well we haven't brought anything much with us. Anybody got any food?
Ben I've got a packet of crisps.
Barry What flavour?
Ben Beef and tomato.

Bacillus roars angrily

Bacillus This one will do. (*Pointing at Ben*)
Chris Do for what?
Bacillus (*roaring*) My feast!
Rob He wants to *eat* Ben?
Matt That's ridiculous.
Steve Well, I think we should at least discuss it.
Gary There are seven of us. We should be able to get past him.
Ben I don't know. Those horns look vicious.

They skirmish with Bacillus but are always wary of the horns and fall back. Suddenly Barry appears with a red matador's cloak and sword. He "bull-fights" Bacillus and kills him. Roars from crowd. Hats and flowers fly onto the stage. He bows

Barry Thank you. Thank you. (*To a girl in audience*) Senorita, with your permission, I dedicate this bull to your beauty!
Gary Look here.
Ben What?
Gary It's a tin of paint.
Chris So?
Gary It might be useful?
Rob We're not going decorating.
Barry No, he's right. This is Dungeons and Dragons, right? There are always things lying around. You pick them up 'cos they're always useful later on.

He picks up the tin of paint

Rob What a load of bull.

Growl from Bacillus. They all jump

    Come on.

They stride on as before

Song 12 (*reprise*): **This Will Be Our Quest**

All (*singing*)   Devils, demons, death and darkness

Put our courage to the test
To seek the Silver Sword of Sagar
This will be our quest

Journeying with joy for justice
Proudly pledged to do our best
Never-ceasing, nor retreating
This will be our quest

Steve holds up his hands to stop them

Steve Hold on. Hold on. Where are we going?
Rob Forest of Nightmares.
Gary Swamp of Doom.
Ben Black Valley of the Night Creatures.
Matt River of Tranquility.
Chris Mountain of Terror.
Barry Sainsbury's.
Rob We've been through all this.
Matt At some length.
Steve No. No. You're not following me.
Ben No. We don't, do we? We all stand in line side by side and we sing the song.

They stride on

All (*singing*)   Devils, demons, death and darkness
Put our courage to the test
To seek the Silver Sword of Sagar
This will be our quest.

Force to flight the foes of freedom
We won't leave it to the rest
Striving, struggling, seeking, searching
This will be our quest.

Steve stops them again, interrupting the second verse

Steve No. Wait. Wait. What I *mean* is, we don't have the map any more. So how do we know where we're going? This is like a labyrinth.
Chris I can remember the map. From here we go east.
Ben West.
Chris Then once we get through the forest we ... What do you mean "west"?
Ben I remember the map. From here we go west.
Chris No. East. Then once we get through the forest we take the right hand fork.
Gary Left.
Chris That will bring us to the edge of the ... What do you mean "left"?
Gary We take the left hand fork. I studied the map very carefully.
Chris No. The right. That brings us to the edge of the ravine. We climb with great care down the steep and narrow path.

Rob Up.

Chris Then we cross the ravine on the . . . What do you mean "up"?

Rob I memorised the map. We climb with great care *up* the steep and narrow path.

Chris No. Down.

Steve This is ridiculous. We're lost.

Chris No it's quite simple. It's east . . .

Ben West.

Chris Then right . . .

Gary Left.

Chris . . . and down.

Rob Up.

Chris East.

Ben West.

Chris Right.

Gary Left.

Chris Down.

Rob Up.

Ben It is *this* way. (*He goes to the right of stage*)

Chris No. Follow me. (*He goes to the left of the stage*)

Steve and Barry remain in the middle. Rob, Gary and Matt go with Chris

Ben exits R

Chris, Rob, Garry and Matt exit L

Barry You shouldn't go off on your own. Ben! Chris, wait a minute!

Steve What should we do?

Barry We'd better go with Ben.

Steve I don't think we should split up.

Creepy noises build up in the background

Barry We already have. Come on.

Steve and Barry follow Ben

Pause

Chris, Rob, Gary and Matt appear at the back of the stage

Chris This is where we take the right fork.

Gary Honestly, Chris, it was the left. I'm sure.

Chris Right!

Gary I'm going left.

Chris That's wrong, but if you are, you shouldn't go alone.

Matt I'll go with Gary.

Chris OK. When you don't reach the ravine, follow us. We'll wait for you there.

They split up, and exit. Steve, Barry and Ben enter at the rear of the stage and exit: Matt and Gary cross the stage. Chris and Rob cross the stage. Steve, Barry and Ben enter

Creepy noises are heard. Ben looks round anxiously

Ben I think it's just possible that I may have made a mistake.
Steve Not to worry, Ben. We can turn round and go back.
Barry If we run we'll soon catch the others up.

They turn and run to the back of the stage. Ben stops, falls backwards and makes choking noises. An invisible creature has attacked him. Barry and Steve run over to him

Barry What is it? A fit?

Barry and Steve both stagger and are felled by blows from this invisible creature. (The creature is hidden from our view by a black cloth which is slowly dropped later in the action to reveal him as the paint spray hits him)

Steve (*reeling from the blow*) What is it?
Barry (*getting up*) Something hit me. It was just like a fist in the . . . (*He flies backwards*)
Ben (*getting up*) But there's nothing here. (*He doubles up*)
Barry There's something here all right, but it's invisible. (*He falls*)

Ben and Steve get up and have their heads banged together. Loud laughter is heard from the invisible creature. Barry starts to crawl off L, but is dragged back by his feet (rope from wings R). The fight continues. All three lie on the floor, defeated. The creature's voice is heard over the loud speakers

Creature (*off*) And now, prepare to die!

A huge axe "floats" in the air, wielded by the creature

Ben Help!
Barry Now we know where it is. Quick! The paint.
Steve What do you mean?
Barry Throw it at it.

Steve throws the paint. The creature appears as the paint hits him. The three attack and defeat it

Steve I think we should have stayed with the others. Let's go back that way.

They exit

Matt and Gary enter

Gary I shouldn't have left our Barry. If he gets into trouble, me mum'll kill me.
Matt I don't think you need to worry about that.
Gary Why not?
Matt Because, what with the Forest of Nightmares, the Swamp of Doom and the Mountain of Terror, your mother's never going to see you again!
Gary Actually, it's the Forest of Doom and the Swamp of . . .

A Gripper appears. This consists of two sheets sewn together with an operator inside

What's that?
Matt I think it's alive.

Loud roar from the Gripper

Gary Help! We're being menaced by a demented tea bag.
Matt It doesn't look too dangerous.

The Gripper turns around revealing a vicious-looking mouth

Gary You were saying?
Matt That's his little perforation. It lets the flavour flood ...

The Gripper leaps on him and wraps itself around him

Gary I think he likes you.

Matt screams, being completely enveloped. Gary tries to help but doesn't know where to begin. The Gripper stands up. It has "eaten" Matt (Matt is inside with the operator)

Matt! Where are you? Oh really, this is ridiculous. It is just not cool to be eaten by a bedsheet.

The Gripper approaches Gary menacingly

No. Just a minute. Stop there. Look on your shoulder. You've got a loose thread. (*He pulls the thread*)

There is a horrendous squeal from the Gripper. It writhes in agony as Gary pulls the long thread out. It collapses to the floor and dies. Gary peeps into its mouth

Matt, are you there?

Matt emerges covered in slime

Matt Oh thanks, Gary. You've saved my life. I was really in the sheet there.
Gary It's too dangerous for just the two of us. We need to find Chris and the others.

Matt and Gary exit

Chris and Rob enter

Rob Are you sure this is the right way?
Chris Quite certain.
Rob But what about the others? How will we find them again?
Chris We'll worry about that when we've done what we came here to do and found the Silver Sword of Sagar.
Rob But just the two of us. We could never do it, could we?
Chris No, but we could try!

Rob looks very confused

Rob No, but we could try?
Chris Yes.

Rob Even if it's impossible?
Chris Yes.
Rob Not the tiniest hope of success?
Chris Yes.
Rob Still go on?
Chris Yes.
Rob That's complete stupidity.
Chris It's the British way!
Rob You're right.

A Giant enters

Chris and Rob shrink back

What is it?
Chris I don't know but it might be friendly.
Giant Who are you who enter the lands of my forefathers? Only one fate awaits any stranger who dares to pass this way—a painful death.
Rob I'd rate him low on friendliness.
Chris Well, if he's going to take that tone, we'll just have to overpower him.
Rob OK. Fine. Overpower him. Er, you go first.

Chris approaches the Giant. Giant points a finger at him. There is a crackle. Chris reels as if from a blow. He advances again. The Giant waves his other hand at him. He flies back

What is it? Bad breath?
Chris Come on. We have to get past him.

The action is repeated with both Rob and Chris ending up on the floor

Any ideas?
Rob Give up?
Giant And now—you die!!! (*He points at each of them*)

Crackles. Flashes. They writhe

Steve, Barry and Ben enter from the wings and Matt and Gary enter through the auditorium.

They attack the Giant but he points at them and they fall. Lots of noise, screams, crackles. All seven lie helpless

Barry There's only one chance.
Other 6 Shut up, Barry!
Barry No, listen. He can overpower us one by one but if we *all* attack at the same time . . .
Giant Ha, ha, ha, ha! Look at these insects squirm!
Chris OK. On the count of three. One, two . . .

Steve starts towards the Giant and is thrown back

No! Together. *Exactly* on the count of three. One. Two. Three.

They attack and defeat the Giant

Ben It worked. Well done, Barry.

Barry is staring into the auditorium in a trance

What's the matter? Barry! What are you looking at?

He turns to the auditorium and gasps. Others turn too. They are looking at a sword dangling from the balcony (or other suitable place)

Steve That's it!
Barry The Silver Sword of Sagar!

They slowly approach and take it

Chris We've done it!

They admire the sword

And now we must return it to the Elflings. I hope we get there in time.

Song 12 (*reprise*): **This Has Been (Will Be) Our Quest**

Chris Rob *(together)*	Journeying with joy for justice Proudly pledged to do our best Never-ceasing, nor retreating This has been our quest.
Steve Gary *(together)*	Light the lamp of liberation Let it shine from east to west Dedicated to our duty This has been our quest.
Matt Ben Barry *(together)*	Force to flight the foes of freedom We won't leave it to the rest Striving, struggling, seeking, searching This has been our quest.
All	Devils, demons, death and darkness Put our courage to the test To seek the Silver Sword of Sagar This has been our quest Our quest Our quest This has been our quest.

They exit

SCENE 5

The Elfling Camp

The Elflings all sit around a dais, applauding

Chief And now, Elflings, we reach the climax of our annual Cherry Blossom Festival. This year the mime contest has been more thrilling than any I can remember. Our first finalist is last year's supreme champion. Your appreciation, please, for Garbo!

Garbo climbs onto the dais. Applause

And his opponent, a newcomer whose performance has been remarkable in this his very first year in the competition—Limbo!

Limbo goes to the dais. Applause

The contest will consist of three rounds. Each contestant will be given one of the subjects on this list and will present his mimed interpretation of it. Garbo step forward.

Garbo steps forward

Your subject is "Eternity".

Garbo remains still for about thirty seconds, then bows. Applause and some Elflings hold up cards saying nine point six, nine point two etc

Limbo, your subject is "Agony".

Limbo takes centre stage

An Orc enters, unseen by the Elflings, and throws a knife which sticks into Limbo's back. He then exits

Limbo writhes, but does not turn. The Elflings, therefore, do not see the knife. After thirty seconds Limbo collapses. There is thunderous applause. Scores of "ten" from all judges

The Orcs and Znakbar rush in

The Elflings leap up, but are surrounded

Znakbar (*to the Chief*) This is your last chance. The Ring of Magor or you die.
Chief We have it not.

Znakbar pauses, looking round at the trembling Elflings

Znakbar DESTROY THEM!

Although outnumbered by Elflings, the Orcs start to wipe them out as the Elflings do not resist

Chris appears with the Sword and leaps on to the dais

Chris Elflings! The Silver Sword of Sagar!

He throws the sword to the Chief who catches it

Chief Let us drive these barbarians from our land!

Song 13: Fight! Fight! Fight!

Dragons   Fight! Fight! Fight!
I smash you or you smash me
Fight! Fight! Fight!

        It's the new morality.

Chris   When you've tried negotiating 'til the middle of the night
        When you've worked out twenty treaties and still haven't
           got it right
        When you've looked into the future and it's not a pretty
           sight
        Then you know that you are gonna have to fight

Dragons Fight! Fight! Fight!
        History has turned a page
        Fight! Fight! Fight!
        It's the spirit of the age.

Chief   When they say they won't attack you but it looks as if they
           might
        When you're backed into a corner and the situation's tight
        When it isn't going to help to say that you are in the right
        Kick and punch and push and prod and pound and bite!

        Fight! Fight! Fight!
        Dump your scruples. No one cares.
        Fight! Fight! Fight!
        Peace and love went out with flares.

Repeat final chorus

The fight continues. Orcs are all killed

Znakbar sneaks off and hides in the audience

Chris The victory is yours.
Chief They will attack us no more. We have destroyed them all. May they
rest in peace.
Barry What about Znakbar? I don't see him.

They all look round the bodies

Chris He cannot have gone far. Where can he be? Can anyone find
Znakbar?

Audience reveal Znakbar's hiding place

Ben There he is. Down there. Look. Grab him.

Elflings rush into the audience

Znakbar slips out

*Elflings grab a member of the audience by mistake and try to drag him onto the
stage*

Chris No. Put him down. Put him down. Does he look like Znakbar, the
most evil slimy creature in all creation?
Barry There's more than a passing resemblance, if you ask me.
Other 6 Shut up, Barry.

The audience member is released

Chris And now we must leave.

Chief Words cannot express our thanks. You will all live forever in the legends of our people.

Garbo Why do you not stay here and live with us?

Chris No. We have our own lives to lead. And you do not need us any more.

Garbo There may come others like Znakbar to threaten our peaceful existence.

Rob Well, you know what to do about it now, don't you? Fight them.

Chris When we have gone, you will have to be your own heroes.

Song 5 (*reprise*): **This Is Your Chance To Be Heroes**

Dragons   Grab this opportunity
                  (You can be a hero)
                  Be what you were meant to be
                  (Not one of the zeroes)
                  This is your chance to be the heroes of your lives.

                  Don't ignore the summons when
                  You can be a hero
                  It's a chance won't come again
                  Not one of the zeroes
                  This is your chance to be the heroes of your lives.

                  Don't ignore the summons when
                  You can be a hero
                  It's a chance won't come again
                  Not one of the zeroes
                  This is your chance to be the heroes of your lives.

Lots of waving etc.

The Seven leave as the Elflings sing on

Black-out

SCENE 6

Changing-Room

There is the sound of the shower running. Rob enters carrying Chris's clothes

Rob OK. Chris. We'll let you off. Here's your clothes back. Chris! He can't still be in the shower? Chris!

Rob goes into the shower

Chris!

Rob re-appears supporting Chris

Chris Oh, my head!

Rob What happened?

Chris I don't know. I must have slipped. Last thing I remember we'd just waved goodbye to the Elflings in the Blossom Marshes and . . . er . . .

Rob Elflings? Blossom Marshes?

Chris Yes. You know.

Rob Never heard of them. What division are they in?

Chris No. The *Elflings!*

Rob I'm sorry. I can't place them.

Chris Oh no. Don't say I . . . a dream . . . while I was unconscious. Oh no, please, please don't say that, *please!*

Rob Why not?

Chris Because it's the corniest ending for a play you could possibly imagine. And it means I'm not really a hero after all. Tell me I am a hero, Rob.

Rob OK, Chris, you're a hero. Let's just get you dressed and then we'd better get a doctor to look at that head of yours. Bangs on the head can do funny things you know.

Rob leads Chris out . . .

Chris We defeated all the Orcs, Rob, you and me and Steve and the others. We were terrific. The Elflings thought we were their legendary heroes and we . . .

They have almost left the stage

Znakbar then appears from the shower shaking water from his clothes

Znakbar What kind of a place is this where it rains indoors?

Chris Look! Look!

Rob Who is it?

Chris Znakbar! I told you. It wasn't a dream. Look.

Znakbar looks around, and at the audience

Znakbar Extraordinary. Inhabitants appear to be imbecilic. You're laughing on the other sides of your faces now, aren't you? Sat there watching me killing the Elflings without batting an eyelid. Well now it's your turn. Ladies and gentlemen, you are all mincemeat. And don't say I didn't warn you!

Song 8 (*reprise*): I Am (We'll Be) Back

They beat me last time
But now I am back
I'm here and now I'm
Back on the attack.

Back!
My survival powers are quite mysterious
Back!
Now I'm back to show *this* world what fear is
Back!

        Now I'm back you'll have to take me serious
        Back!
        Yes, now I'm back.

Two policemen and two men in white coats enter and approach Chris and Rob

Police 1 Have either of you seen a man about five foot, wearing leather, studs, chains, ratty hair, ugly?

Chris Yes. There. It's Znakbar.

Police 2 Rodney Bugsworth.

Police 1 Third time he's escaped this year. He'll have to go into the high security wing.

Znakbar   Back
        My survival powers are quite mysterious
        Back!
        Now I'm back to show *this* world what fear is
        Back!
        Now I'm back you'll have to take me serious
        Back!
        Yes, now I'm back.

Police 1 OK, Rodney, these gentlemen from the hospital have come to take you back.

Chris Be careful. He can be vicious.

Police 2 No, son. He's harmless. Just gets a little over-excited.

Chris But ...

Znakbar hits policeman 2. The men in white coats go after Znakbar

Police 2   Back!
        Take him back and tranquilise him well, then
        Back!
        Throw him back into his padded cell, men
Police 1   Back!
        Tender care for the mentally unwell, when
        Back!
        When we get back

They drag Znakbar off stage, struggling

Chris But that was Znakbar!

Rob No, Chris. It's that bang on your head.

In the background the rest of the cast begin to sing faintly. It grows louder under the following

Chris But it was real, Rob. In a way it was real. The quest. Freedom. Justice. Liberation. They're not dreams, Rob. They're real. We have to fight for them.

Others come forward and all join in singing

Song 12 (*reprise*): **This Will Be Our Quest**

All

Journeying with joy for justice
Proudly pledged to do our best
Never-ceasing, nor retreating
This will be our quest.

Light the lamp of liberation
Let it shine from east to west
Dedicated to our duty
This will be our quest.

Force to fight the foes of freedom
We won't leave it to the rest
Striving, struggling, seeking, searching
This will be our quest

Force to fight the foes of freedom
We won't leave it to the rest
Striving, struggling, seeking, searching
This will be our quest
Our quest
Our quest
This has been our quest.

CURTAIN

FURNITURE AND PROPERTY LIST

ACT I

SCENE 1

On stage: Flutes, baskets, paint, paint brushes, paint board

Personal: **Snorc:** weapon

SCENE 2

On stage: Box, pair of tongs, "a fire beetle"

SCENE 3

On stage: Shower unit

Personal: **Gazebo:** ring

SCENE 4

Off stage: Stepladder, fire buckets, water bombs

Personal: **Znakbar:** water pistol, soda siphon

SCENE 6

On stage: 2 fishing rods

SCENE 7

Personal: **Chris:** ring

SCENE 8

On stage: Clothes shop cubicle, underpants

SCENE 10

On stage: Aeroplane flight deck
Microphone
Maps

Personal: **Pilot 2:** clipboard

SCENE 11

Personal: **Chris:** ring

SCENE 12

Personal: **Orcs:** weapons

ACT II

SCENE 1

On stage: Rope, blackboard, chalk, a lettuce, apple, tub of butter, paintbrush, paint

Personal: **Znakbar:** stick, cord, knife, matches

SCENE 2

Off stage: Dusty book, scroll, chest. *In it:* papers, extraordinary items **(Wakelam)**

Personal: **Steve:** map
Wakelam: candle

SCENE 3

On stage: Tin of paint

Off stage: Red matador's cloak, sword **(Barry)**
Hats, flowers (*Stage Management*)
Axe **(Creature)**

Personal: **Steve:** map
Matt: matches

SCENE 4

On stage: Low platform (*dais*)

Personal: **An Orc:** knife
Chris: sword

SCENE 5

On stage: Shower unit (as Act I, Scene 3)

LIGHTING PLOT

ACT I

ACT I, SCENE 1

To open: Exterior lighting

Cue 1 **Orcs** hurry Crobo off   (Page 2)
        Black-out

ACT I, SCENE 2

To open: Exterior lighting

Cue 2 **Elflings** gather round body of Crobo   (Page 5)
        Fade to black-out

ACT I, SCENE 3

To open: Interior lighting

Cue 3 **All** disappear   (Page 6)
        Black-out

ACT I, SCENE 4

To open: Interior lighting

Cue 4 **Znakbar** soaks **Orcs** with water   (Page 9)
        Black-out

ACT I, SCENE 5

To open: Exterior lighting

Cue 5 **Elflings** carry Chris out   (Page 11)
        Black-out

ACT I, SCENE 6

To open: Exterior lighting

Cue 6 **Chris** (*singing*): ". . . heroes of our lives."   (Page 13)
        Black-out

ACT I, SCENE 7

To open: Interior lighting

Cue 7   **Rob** edges out of church   (Page 15)
           Black-out

ACT I, SCENE 8
To open: Interior lighting
Cue 8   **Chris** (*singing*): "... heroes of our lives."   (Page 16)
           Black-out

ACT I, SCENE 9
To open: Interior lighting
Cue 9   **Znakbar** (*singing*): "... could be like me."   (Page 18)
           Black-out

ACT I, SCENE 10
To open: Interior lighting
Cue 10   **Pilots** burst into tears   (Page 21)
           Black-out

ACT I, SCENE 11
To open: Exterior lighting
Cue 11   **Crowd** disappears   (Page 22)
           Black-out

ACT I, SCENE 12
To open: Exterior lighting
Cue 12   **Znakbar** (*singing*): "You've seen the last of me." (Page 26)
           Black-out

                                  ACT II

ACT II, SCENE 1
To open: Exterior lighting
Cue 13   At end of song 9   (Page 31)
           Black-out

ACT II, SCENE 2

To open: Interior lighting
Cue 14   **Elflings** fade into background   (Page 35)
           Black-out

ACT II, SCENE 3

To open: Dim lighting

Cue 15   **Owl** hoots   (Page 36)
            Darken lights

Cue 16   At end of song 12   (Page 40)
            Black-out

ACT II, SCENE 4

To open: General lighting

Cue 17   **All** (singing): "This has been our quest."   (Page 47)
            Black-out

ACT II, SCENE 5

To open: Exterior lighting

Cue 18   The seven leave, the **Elflings** sing on   (Page 50)
            Black-out

ACT II, SCENE 6

To open: Interior lighting

No cues

EFFECTS PLOT

ACT I

Cue 1	As Scene 3 opens *Sound of a shower running*	(Page 5)
Cue 2	The **elflings** touch the ring *Flash, smoke*	(Page 6)
Cue 3	**Trumbo:** ". . . courage of our ancestors." *Flash*	(Page 10)
Cue 4	As Scene 7 opens *Choir singing*	(Page 13)
Cue 5	As Scene 10 opens *Aircraft noise throughout scene*	(Page 18)
Cue 6	**Pilot 2:** "Oh, no!" *Plane nose dives, then is controlled*	(Page 19)
Cue 7	**Pilots** finish song *Plane nose dives, then is controlled*	(Page 21)

ACT II

Cue 8	As Scene 3 opens *A howling wind; owls hoot, wolves howl*	(Page 36)
Cue 9	**Barry:** ". . . full of hedgehogs." *Howls*	(Page 36)
Cue 10	**Chris:** ". . . quicken our pace." *Howls*	(Page 36)
Cue 11	**Chris:** "Stream! Stream! Stream! *A splash of water; howls*	(Page 36)
Cue 12	**Steve:** "I don't think we should split up." *Creepy noises build up*	(Page 43)
Cue 13	**Giant** points a finger at **Chris** *Crackle. Repeat as necessary*	(Page 46)
Cue 14	**Giant:** "And now—you die." *Crackles, flashes*	(Page 46)
Cue 15	**Giant** points at other five Dragons *Crackles, continuing*	(Page 46)
Cue 16	As Scene 6 opens *Sound of a shower running*	(Page 50)

MADE AND PRINTED IN GREAT BRITAIN BY
LATIMER TREND & COMPANY LTD PLYMOUTH
MADE IN ENGLAND

Lightning Source UK Ltd.
Milton Keynes UK
UKOW06f0835260416

272983UK00016B/447/P